IMAGES OF THE FUTURE

IMAGES OF THE FUTURE

ALAN K. WALTZ

Ezra Earl Jones, Editor

ABINGDON   Nashville

Images of the Future

*Copyright © 1980
by The General Council on Ministries
of The United Methodist Church*

All rights reserved.
No part of this book may be reproduced in any manner whatsoever without written permission of the publisher except brief quotations embodied in critical articles or reviews. For information address Abingdon, Nashville, Tennessee.

Library of Congress Cataloging in Publication Data

WALTZ, ALAN K.
  Images of the future.
  (Into our third century)
  1. United Methodist Church (United States) I. Title. II. Series.
BX8382.2.W34   287'673   79-25028

ISBN 0-687-18689-7

Lines from "The People, Yes" by Carl Sandburg, published in *Complete Poems*, are reprinted by permission of Harcourt Brace Jovanovich, Inc. © 1950.

MANUFACTURED BY THE PARTHENON PRESS AT
NASHVILLE, TENNESSEE, UNITED STATES OF AMERICA

To

Dorothy C. and Murray H. Leiffer

Contents

FOREWORD /9

CHAPTER 1 /13
Introduction

CHAPTER 2 /20
Expectations for the Denomination

CHAPTER 3 /27
Theological and Value Issues Facing
the United Methodist Church

CHAPTER 4 /32
Relationship Between the Local Church and
Other Levels of the Denomination

CHAPTER 5 /41
Impact of Economic Issues

CHAPTER 6 /49
Expectations of and for Leadership

CHAPTER 7 /57
Organizational Issues Before the Denomination

CHAPTER 8 /65
Criteria for Assessing Future Directions

CHAPTER 9 /70
Images of the Future

APPENDICES /75-77

NOTES /79

Foreword

In 1984 United Methodism will observe the 200th anniversary of the Christmas Conference of 1784—the date most often regarded as the beginning of the Methodist movement in the United States. We shall pause to remember how the Wesleyan vision of holy love and active piety spread like an unquenchable flame as the United States expanded from coast to coast, how people of all races, cultures, and classes rallied to a gospel offering salvation and demanding good works as the fruit of Christian faith in God.

But we shall do more. Our bicentennial is also a time to soberly anticipate the future, to take stock of ourselves as we move into our third century. Our inheritance is rich in faith and works. It nourishes us, but our tasks are now, and tomorrow. The United Methodist Church is large (9.7 million members in the United States), still highly visible and active, but some indicators of our future prospects are disturbing. We shall reflect on and discuss these concerns as United Methodists until we once again catch a vision of ministry and service that is worthy of our past, builds upon our present, and thrusts us again into the mainstream of human life with the message of God's redeeming love.

You, a United Methodist lay member or pastor, and your congregation have a vital role in both the celebration and the search. It is the people in the pews and pulpits of United Methodism who must reestablish our identity and purpose through discussion on who we are as United Methodists, what we wish to accomplish, and how we pursue our goals in the years ahead.

A Research Design for United Methodism as It Enters Its Third Century, initiated by the General Council on Ministries with the encouragement of the Council of Bishops, is intended to support your efforts. It is an extensive study of selected issues of fundamental ministry and organizational concern to the denomination and a study of the environment in which United Methodism in the United States serves. Over a four year period, beginning in 1980, eighteen separate volumes are being released for your use. The present book *Images of the Future* is the second volume in the series and a companion to *The Church in a Changing Society,* also being released this year. *In Praise of Learning,* a unique view of Christian education, will be released soon. Subsequent volumes will deal with the present realities and future form, content, and/or challenges of outreach ministry (mission, evangelism, and social witness), social movements and issues, church leadership and management, non-parish institutions (for example, colleges, hospitals, homes, community centers), local churches as community institutions, women in church and society, ecumenical relationships, ethnic minority constituencies, understanding faith (the role of theology), professional ministry, general agencies, financial support, and polity (the philosophy and form of church government and the organization).

The General Council on Ministries commends to you now this volume by Alan K. Waltz. It summarizes the informed judgment of United Methodist church leaders about the world in which our denomination will find itself in the next decade and at the end of the twentieth century. The book also images the probable and appropriate responses of United Methodism to its environment across the next two decades. See if you

FOREWORD

agree. Share your reflections within your own congregation, with other Christians, and with district, conference, and general church leaders. Your response will also be welcomed by the members and staff of the council.

Norman E. Dewire
General Secretary

Ezra Earl Jones
Editor

The General Council on Ministries
601 West Riverview Avenue
Dayton, Ohio 45406

April, 1980

CHAPTER 1

Introduction

Purpose of the Book

The purpose of this book is to stimulate serious consideration of the future prospects of The United Methodist Church so that we may be prepared to meet our Christian responsibilities as appropriately as possible in the future.

Society is constantly undergoing change. The increasing diversity among United Methodists reflects the diversity in all aspects of society. Important concerns have been voiced by many segments of our denomination: How can past form and practices maintain community and unity in The United Methodist Church? What should be our goals as people of God, and how are they to be manifested? What new concepts can we use to fulfill God's will in the future, and what rationales will support the decisions that will determine these new concepts? The mood is not one of finding ways to justify continuance of programs and institutions developed in the past. Rather, it is one of seeking creative ways in which every segment of the denomination can fulfill its task in the months and years ahead.

As Christians we affirm the past and continuing work of Christ as we strive to preserve our common heritage and to understand its meaning in today's world. We are called upon to remain focused on God and the eternal consummation while at the same time being Christ's servants and witnesses in our world. John Wesley puts our task in perspective.

> Walking now with joy and not with fear, in a clear, steady sight of things eternal, we shall look on pleasure, wealth, praise, all things of

earth, as bubbles upon the water, counting nothing important, nothing desirable, nothing worth a deliberate thought but only what is "within the veil" where Jesus "sitteth at the right hand of God."[1]

The challenge is to use our God-given resources to evangelize the spirit, heal the body, and inform the mind. Yet we are becoming increasingly aware that in order to comprehend and fulfill God's will in future society, *we must become more knowledgeable and concerned about the forces and events shaping that future.*

A 1970 report of the National Industrial Conference Board succinctly stated the case for understanding the nature and impact of future events.

> The explosive growth of science and technology is increasing the rate and scale, and altering the character, of social change so fast that plans and programs are outdated before they are implemented. Without more accurate long-range forecasts, key decision-makers in business and government are "backing into the future." This invites serious threats to their own and the public interest.[2]

Dr. George Sawyer, a professor of management, speaks of forecasting and studying the future. "The . . . reason for attempting to forecast changes in markets and society is to gain sufficient lead time before each event so that management can take effective action in advance."[3] In order for The United Methodist Church to respond appropriately to future society in terms of our faith, we *must* become informed about and study the emerging trends and directions of society. If we do not seek to understand the forces and events shaping the future and make the necessary decisions while as wide a range of options as possible is still available, trends and events will of themselves create the actions and reactions.

The approaching 1984 bicentennial of The United Methodist Church in the United States provides a significant time for the denomination to reflect not only on its past two hundred years, but also on its future in the remaining years of the twentieth century. Yet even if this event were not immediately before us, the concern and issues facing the denomination would still require serious reflection and assessment of the future.

This book does not purport to prescribe a set of actions to be implemented before The United Methodist Church can fulfill its destiny and task in the years ahead. Nor do we attempt herein to provide a definitive analysis of future trends and issues. The volume presents data to stimulate individual reflection and facilitate informed discussion so that we may perceive the emerging environment and take appropriate steps to best utilize the available resources in the future. To fail to do so would be to find ourselves in a situation described by Carl Sandburg in "The People, Yes."

> He took the wheel in a lashing roaring hurricane
> And by what compass did he steer the cause of the ship?
> "My policy is to have no policy," he said in the early months,
> And three years later, "I have been controlled by events."

Sources of Data

Data presented have been obtained from four studies. The first and primary study, conducted at the end of 1978 and early 1979, utilized the Delphi forecasting technique (named after the "Oracle of Delphi," which was believed by the ancient Greeks to be able to foresee the future). This is a relatively new method of presenting a set of propositions to a group of people knowledgeable in the subject being studied and developing from their responses a consensus as to the probability and effect of the future occurrence of those propositions. Initial responses are tabulated, summarized, and returned to the participants, who are asked to respond again to the propositions after reviewing their answers alongside the statistically combined responses of the group. The final opinions of individual members are then statistically averaged to reach a group opinion. The Delphi technique is more fully described in Appendix A.

In this study, participants were carefully selected to include individuals representing the wide range of perspectives, experience, and interests within The United Methodist Church. Diverse representation was sought in the areas of age, sex, race, and ethnic background, and jurisdiction, ministerial, and lay status. A list of groups represented is given in Appendix B.

A series of 122 propositions concerning society in general and The United Methodist Church in particular were sent to the participants. These persons were asked to assess each statement on a five-point scale for each of three responses: (1) the desirability of the occurrence of the proposition for The United Methodist Church, (2) the probability of its occurrence by 1984, and (3) the probability of its occurrence by the year 2000.

Because of the techniques used in a Delphi study and the careful selection of knowledgeable participants, the net result is not idle speculation, but is based on informed judgment and insight.

The second study was conducted by the General Council on Ministries in the fall of 1978. Selected local church pastors, local church and annual conference lay leadership, and all directors of the annual conference Council on Ministries were invited to participate. By means of a questionnaire, research was done to determine these local church leaders' views as to the key trends, issues, and needs which will face the local church, annual conference, and the denomination between now and 1984.

The third source of data was a Harris public opinion poll as to non-United Methodists' attitudes and opinions concerning The United Methodist Church. This study was commissioned by the General Council on Ministries in the fall of 1978 and the findings were released in the spring of 1979.

Finally, data were drawn from William Ramsden's review of social, economic, demographic, and other trends in the United States and their potential impacts on The United Methodist Church. This work is also being published in 1980 by Abingdon under the title *The Church in a Changing Society*.

Our intent is not to overwhelm the reader with large quantities of data. We desire simply to present sufficient background information to illuminate the topic, note the projected trends, suggest implications, and assist the reader to reflect on their meaning for The United Methodist Church.

Acknowledgments

This project was conducted under the auspices and direction of The General Council on Ministries of The United Methodist Church. Throughout the study guidance and counsel were received from many individuals and groups. Members of the Advisory Committee on Research, an adjunct group of council, collectively and individually reviewed the design of the project and suggested many helpful improvements. We are indebted to these persons for their insightful comments.

One hundred thirty-three persons participated in the total process as members of the Delphi panel. In responding to two rounds of inquiries, they gave freely of their time and interest. As church leaders at the local, annual conference, and national levels, they expressed their hopes, concerns, and projections for the denomination. We are deeply grateful for the voluntary participation of these people without whose candid responses this project could not have been completed.

The manuscript was written during a portion of a study leave granted by The General Council on Ministries. Without this period of relatively uninterrupted time, it would have been quite difficult for me to complete the text.

I owe a particular debt of gratitude for the wise counsel and encouragement of my colleagues on the staff of the council. Gerald Clapsaddle, Norman Dewire, Edith Goodwin, Ezra Earl Jones, and Leonard Miller have all helped significantly. Ezra Earl Jones has been of inestimable assistance not only with methodological and research aspects of the work, but also through his editorial counsel and guidance. Carol Evans Smith assisted significantly with the editing of the final manuscript. Mrs. Lola Conrad deserves a special word of thanks for her superior handling of many details of the project, including tabulating responses and typing several versions of the manuscript. Velva Hardaway also assisted in the preparation of the final manuscript. Any deficiencies of the study or its presentation must be attributed not to these people, but to me.

All books take considerable time and energy from the author. These same elements, in different ways, are taken from the author's family as well. Mary Joyce and our children have been exceptionally tolerant and gracious of the time and energies diverted from them to this book. Their love, understanding, and support have been especially important while I struggled with the manuscript.

The book is dedicated to two beloved friends and teachers whose impact on my life has been enormous. The influence of Dorothy and Murray Leiffer on theological students and on the life of this denomination for over fifty years has been immeasurable. Few in The United Methodist Church have done more to foster understanding of its life and character or to move it into the future with purpose and resolve.

A Charge to the Reader

In our assessment of the information provided in this book, we realize that as the rate of change accelerates, time for data collection, analysis, and planning diminishes. We may discover that we are using criteria and standards of judgment that are

INTRODUCTION

outdated. We may realize that whereas we have been accustomed to dealing with each problem, issue, and administrative decision separately, the current need is for an integrated analysis of the issues. We may hear demands for immediate solutions and sense an impatience with solutions which take time.

There is increased competition for scarce resources—not energy and natural resources alone, but funds, time, and commitment as well. There are uncertainties in both direction and perception of leadership. We must realize that we are living in a time of transition, if transition has not indeed become the constant state.

In truth, yours is the greatest part of this undertaking. Words presented here will not determine the future of the local church, the annual conference, or even the future of the entire denomination. Whether or not The United Methodist Church fulfills its mission in the coming years will depend on the degree to which committed, concerned United Methodists begin to understand what is required and act decisively on the basis of their increased awareness.

The reader is asked to consider carefully the information presented and to explore the impact of the possible occurrence of the forecast. Strive to envision the future toward which the local church, the annual conference, and the entire denomination should direct themselves if they are to fulfill their mission. The charge to you is to approach the information with an inquisitive mind, to deal with it in an open and objective manner, and to discover how the denomination might, with courage and conviction, realize the future you envision for it.

CHAPTER 2

Expectations for the Denomination

The prevailing opinions of the Delphi panel are (1) that many aspects of The United Methodist Church are not functioning well, (2) that future societal and denominational trends will not be in the best interests of The United Methodist Church, and (3) that the denomination may not resolve to overcome the negative effects of these trends. Because the Delphi panel perceived the environment as becoming less and less hospitable to organized religion, the result was an essentially pessimistic assessment of the future of the denomination, that is, if we allow events to run their course without intervention.

This chapter will present forecasts as to participation levels within The United Methodist Church, the role of religion in society, and the denomination's willingness to make changes necessary to respond appropriately to these trends.

The focus is not the individual member's personal religious experience, the local church pastor's work, or even the local congregation, but rather the denomination as a whole.

The Role of Religion in Society

Notwithstanding the goal of the Christian churches to remain a strong and vital influence in American society, most major denominations in the United States have experienced decreases in participation and membership in recent years. The Delphi participants expressed an overwhelming consensus that Christian faith and organized religion will become progressively less influential in United States society during the remainder of this century. Further, surveys of religion in American life, such as those done by the George Gallup organization, also indicate that the impact of Christianity will lessen in the years ahead.[1]

Although religious beliefs are still important to most Americans (according to the Gallup surveys) and most believe that the church can be depended on to be faithful to its basic functions, society's directions seem to be determined more and more by non-religious themes and values. Activities and interests offered by other aspects of our culture are threatening or overriding many people's motivation to participate in traditional church experience.

The Delphi panel projected that participation in all types of voluntary organizations, including organized religion, will become progressively less important in the life of the individual in the United States during the next two decades. Although a 1976 Gallup survey on religion in America reported a slight increase in the proportions of American adults who attend church regularly, the survey also emphasized a trend with disturbing long-range implications: Only 33 percent of Protestants under 30 years of age attended church regularly as contrasted with 44 percent of those age 50 or older.[2] Many young people have never experienced the life and work of a local church, while an increasing number of older persons are surrendering their active roles as local church leaders.

Few of the Delphi panel expect organized religion to play a more influential part in the life of the individual in the future, nor do they expect the level of participation in church activities to increase. Thus, organized religion appears likely to find itself in the midst of a culture not particularly hostile, but increasingly less sympathetic to their teachings, resolutions, and influence. This forecast presents an undisputed challenge to every denomination dealing both with survival in this future climate and service in the name of Christ in the next two decades.

Participation in The United Methodist Church

In keeping with the forecast for the future role of all organized religion in American society, the Delphi panel members forecast the continuance of the decline in membership and participation in various United Methodist activities which have been documented in the past decade. The undesirable trends projected by the Delphi study to occur between now and 1984 in The United Methodist Church are (1) a decrease in the number of people actively involved in local churches, (2) a decrease in the number of people attending local church worship services, (3) a decrease in the number of people involved in church school programs and activities, and (4) more use of non-United Methodist curricula in the church school. There was a high level of consensus that these trends will continue through 1984, with slightly more favorable prospects forecast for the end of the century. For example, the majority believed that by the year 2000 membership would begin to grow, but worship attendance would continue to decrease. A slight increase in church school involvement coupled with an increasing use of non-United Methodist curriculum materials was projected.

In the 1978 survey of local church leadership, two major concerns were revealed: the gradual erosion of membership and participation, and the lack of outreach and evangelism. Growth was clearly viewed as a desirable goal, but there was no expressed expectation of an improvement in the denomination's performance in attracting and retaining members. The need for major emphasis on outreach and evangelism was recommended more often in the context of stemming the decline of the local church than as a primary mission to seek out and fulfill the individual spiritual needs of the unchurched. Yet certainly a failure to develop new forms and methods for outreach, nurture, and service may cause the closing of many local churches, resulting in a loss of service in the name of Christ to members and countless others in the community.

The 1978 Harris poll reported that nearly two-thirds of United Methodists interviewed believed the denomination was growing. If these responses accurately reflect the belief of the average United Methodist, it is apparent that the membership and leadership hold widely differing perceptions of denominational growth. Perhaps this lack of accurate information on the part of the general membership accounts for their reluctance to act on the major problems facing local churches and annual conferences both now and in the future. The membership must be informed that the failure to address these issues at all levels of the denomination may result in a substantial weakening of many programs and ministries, if not the eventual demise of The United Methodist Church.

A Note of Optimism

Positive Public Image of United Methodists Produces Fertile Ground for Outreach. Despite the fact that our society is expected to take less and less of its direction from organized religion, a note of optimism arises from the fact that The United Methodist Church is perceived positively by society as a whole. Because of the responsible and open character of our past service to society, The United Methodist Church does not have a negative public image to overcome in order to render Christian service and influence society in Christ's name during the remaining years of this century.

The Harris poll of non-United Methodists concerning their views of The United Methodist Church revealed that those interviewed see the denomination as (1) open and receptive to new members from all walks of life, (2) concerned about the spiritual well-being of its members, (3) highly influential regarding attitudes and beliefs of its members, and (4) concerned about the poor and minorities. Those with knowledge of The United Methodist Church, particularly the older persons interviewed, approved of its ministry. There were many who knew little about what The United Methodist Church does, but this is understandable in view of the commitment to and interest in other denominations on the part of many of those responding. Where no strong denominational ties were indicated, there appeared to be a willingness to become more involved with a local United Methodist church if additional contacts were made with them from within the church. This willingness was seen to be a result of the open and responsive image of The United Methodist Church.

The Harris poll also discovered that the number of persons who identify themselves with The United Methodist Church is approximately 8 percent of the population, or about double our recorded membership. While a third of this number indicated a strong commitment to a local church, two-thirds reported that they are either inactive or only moderately active in a local church. This reflects a slightly higher level of involvement than was noted for those giving other denominational affiliations. In view of the Delphi panel's expectation of no increase in the number of active participants in The United Methodist Church, the high percentage of the population who said they were related to the denomination may lead us to expect an increase in the number of people marginally related to the denomination in the future.

Thus, The United Methodist Church has a significant number of people, both among those identifying themselves with the denomination and those with no strong denominational ties, who are open to purposeful and meaningful influence from the denomination, but who need active cultivation and outreach from within the local church.

Needed: The Resolve to Change

The Delphi panel has projected for us a future environment in which religion will be considered increasingly less important to the individual and to society. We are faced with a continuing decrease in membership and participation in denominational activities. But the most alarming forecast by the panel is that The United Methodist Church *will lack the will or resolve* to take the steps necessary to prepare itself to be what it hopes to be in the future—a strong and vital influence in American society.

In order for The United Methodist Church to realize that goal, certain steps appear to be prerequisite and were deemed highly desirable by the Delphi panel of knowledgeable United Methodists. The group projects, however, that *without substantial changes in its current experience,* The United Methodist Church is unlikely to resolve to take the following steps.

1) *The development of a clear sense of direction and purpose for its life and work.* The majority of the Delphi panel feel that The United Methodist Church is unlikely to develop even by the year 2000 the sense of direction and identity needed to enable the denomination to marshal its resources and move with vigor toward fulfilling its mission in the years ahead.

2) *The development of a major program of stewardship education for the laity.* Most of the panel did not expect this badly needed program of undergirding our ministry to be undertaken even by the year 2000.

3) *The development of a significant program of outreach and evangelism.* Most panel members do not expect a strong program of outreach and evangelism to be developed even by the year 2000.

4) *The major reallocation of resources to reach those not now members of The United Methodist Church.* Although the vast majority of the panel considered reallocation to be essential to our success in carrying Christ's work to non-members, many did not expect a major reallocation of resources to occur by

1984. There was some optimism about the accomplishment of a reallocation by the year 2000, but 20 percent of the panel believed the denomination would not take this step even by then.

5) *The starting of new congregations by annual conferences.* Although some optimism was expressed that a significant number of new congregations will be started by the year 2000, most panel members do not expect annual conferences to start many new congregations in the near future.

The picture thus presented by the Delphi panel seems to be of a denomination primarily concerned with administering its past and describing the symptoms of its present malaise, but unwilling to seek a better understanding of its discomfort or to take the requisite steps to effect a cure. However, this pessimistic outlook will prevail only if events are allowed to run their course without intervention.

The way we deal with the issues presented in this book will determine the future effectiveness, if not survival, of The United Methodist Church. Some issues presented for discussion are societal matters to which we must respond with clarity and precision. Others are denominational matters requiring careful consideration, appropriate decisions, and consistent administration. The hope for the future is that The United Methodist Church will study and seek to understand its future role in society and resolve to do what is required to prepare itself for that role.

CHAPTER 3

Theological and Value Issues Facing The United Methodist Church

The life and experience of the church are based on its theological and ethical, or moral, principles. A Christian organization, in order to survive, must constantly interpret its theological and moral principles in light of new experiences and modified relationships which alter the character of society. If it is to make a presentation of its theology and moral teachings sufficient to influence its members and society as a whole, a church must seek to understand the meaning of biblical witness and the life and teachings of Christ both for those living in the time when those teachings were presented, and for those living in today's and tomorrow's world.

Rapid changes in moral values and life-styles in America in recent years raise three issues which must be seriously explored by The United Methodist Church:

1) What will be the nature and direction of changes in values and life-styles in the future?
2) What will be the teachings and position of The United Methodist Church regarding these changes?
3) How will the denomination instruct its members as to its position on morality and life-style issues?

Moral Values and Life-Styles: The Future Environment

Life-Style Predictions. The Delphi panel predicted that life-styles will continue to change at a rapid pace. The

continuance of the following trends in the United States was forecast:
1) Increasingly more liberal sexual attitudes
2) A modest but consistent decrease in the importance of the family
3) A decline in sexism, and a movement toward equality for women
4) A placing of a higher priority on "living for today" than on making long-term plans and commitments
5) A placing of more emphasis on the individual's ability to determine his/her own life-style
6) Less importance of work or occupation as a source of an individual's identity and meaning
7) Increasing diversity within society, i.e., more separateness in life-styles among persons in differing racial and ethnic minorities, age groups, and education levels

The Delphi panel expressed mixed reactions as to the desirability of these trends. For example, the panel clearly believes the decline in importance of the family unit is undesirable. The group is essentially neutral as to the desirability of the liberalization of sexual attitudes. Highly favored is the decline in sexism and the enhanced role for women in society.

The study disclosed an interesting ambivalence relating to the other life-style trends noted. The group affirms the ability of individuals to determine their own life-style and to find identity and meaning from areas other than their occupation. Yet at the same time, the panel feels it undesirable for individuals to live only for the moment and for various groups in society to develop increasing separateness in life-styles. Thus, conflict exists between according the individual more freedom and recognizing the need for commonality and cohesiveness within society.

Value Formation. The Christian church has traditionally been the source of theological and moral principles held by Americans. The Delphi panel predicts a grim future for the church in this regard: Although the church will continue to influence the formation of ethical values of Americans, that influence will be a steadily diminishing one. The moral climate will be one in which historically prized values (hard work, sharing with neighbor, strong moral code, etc.) will be held in increasingly low esteem. This decreasing impact of the church on the formation of moral principles is projected to be a major concern of the United Methodist laity in the future.

Thus, as patterns of thought and behavior change radically and as the influence of the Christian church on value formation steadily diminishes, we see an increasingly concerned United Methodist laity searching for guidance and authority in determining moral values and appropriate life-styles, and for a clear interpretation of Christian teachings as applied to these issues. Indeed, those interviewed during the 1978 survey of local church leaders indicated that the most pressing issue facing the local church is how to present the Christian perspective in a world of rapidly changing moral values and life-styles.

In the absence of clear guidance from the denomination in determining moral values and life-styles, there may be a tendency for the individual to "write the church off" as irrelevant to the issues and to turn elsewhere for moral guidance, to the detriment of both the individual and The United Methodist Church.

Impact of the Public Media. Aside from the voice of the church, the most pervasive force presently influencing moral values in the nation is the public media, particularly television. The Delphi panel predicts that the public media will continue to be a major societal force in the future:

1) The public media, especially television, will be the

dominant influence on establishing moral standards and on standards of consumption.

2) Public media presentations by non-United Methodist preachers and evangelists will be increasingly influential on the laity and clergy in The United Methodist Church, particularly in the near future.

The public media is seen by the panel as such a strong and pervasive force in the future that there is little expectation that The United Methodist Church in its traditional role can even compete with the public media as a primary teacher and guide for moral conduct.

United Methodist Theological Perspectives: Future Prospects

A strong wave of religious conservatism is likely to rise in the near future, subsiding slightly by the year 2000, says the majority of the Delphi panel. A majority of the panel considers this undesirable for The United Methodist Church. A third of the respondents were neutral as to the desirability of the conservative trend. Although no consensus emerged as to whether a major Christian revival would be sparked in the conservative denominations in the United States because of this trend, the mood even in the year 2000 is predicted to be still more conservative than now.

The panel also predicted increased diversity of beliefs among both the laity and the denomination as a whole. While almost two-thirds of the panel considered theological diversity desirable for the denomination, only 9 percent saw as desirable such diversity in viewpoint among the laity. The meaning of this ambivalence expressed by the panel is not immediately clear. Perhaps it reflects a tension felt within the denomination throughout its history: while we value the freedom to move toward greater diversity, an actual move in that direction on the part of the laity would not be beneficial to The United Methodist Church.

Prerequisite to United Methodist Influence on Morality of the Nation: Unity

As The United Methodist Church moves into its third century, increasing diversity of interpretation and perspective within the denomination emphasizes a need for unity if we are to influence our members and the nation in the name of Christ. The individual's need for guidance in a rapidly changing society calls for The United Methodist Church to take a clear stand on moral and theological issues based on the spiritual and moral values of the Christian faith. In our striving to fulfill our mission as servants of Christ, we must devote our attention and resources to discussing, articulating, and developing a unified stand to present basic criteria by which an individual can evaluate moral issues and life-style questions and by which the local church, annual conference, and denomination can evaluate leadership, polity, organizational, and financial issues. In the absence of such a unified stand, The United Methodist Church could suffer irreparable damage by forfeiting to the general public and its media the function of determining the morality of our nation.

CHAPTER 4

Relationship Between the Local Church and Other Levels of the Denomination

Confidence in many large institutions of society has been shaken. National and state governments, as well as large industrial organizations, are often viewed as remote, complex, and uncaring. When this attitude is coupled with the increasing trend, noted earlier, of individual self-determination, the result is a national mood of suspicion of large organizations. Even The United Methodist Church appears to be affected by this phenomenon. The Delphi project discloses a shift in emphasis away from denominational or general-level programs and activities toward programs planned at the local level focusing on the life and ministry of the local congregation. This mood is seen in predictions about the way the congregation views its priorities, organizational and resourcing patterns, and requests for accountability and evaluation.

Local Church: Inward Focus

Top Priority: Concerns at Home. While the Delphi panel members believe it is desirable for The United Methodist Church to be closely involved with social issues at all levels, they predict that outreach of ministry and concern beyond the local level will be limited in the near future. The local congregation will find itself increasingly preoccupied with its own problems of institutional maintenance, such as caring for property, supporting the pastor, and meeting the immediate needs of its members, throughout the next two decades, and the majority of the laity and clergy will be involved with social concerns and issues within the local community. Although a substantial interest in national issues is forecast, it will be less than the interest shown for local matters. Global issues will attract the least interest of all, gaining the attention of only a third of the laity in 1984. Thus, for the near future there is projected a decreasing level of interest in and knowledge about social issues in direct proportion to their distance from the local congregation.

Programs Beyond Local Church as Burden and Drain on Resources of Local Congregation. It is projected that, particularly in the near future, the laity will begin to consider programs beyond the local church a burden and a drain on their congregation's resources. This burden is compounded by inflation and increased costs to the local church, a matter which will be discussed further in the next chapter. Thus, a major problem is foreseen in gaining support for programs beyond the local level in the near future.

Gradual Widening of Focus of Local Church by 2000. The panel, by a mild consensus, projected that by the end of the century the local church will reach an enhanced understanding of its role in outreach and ministry beyond its own congregation. The laity may then consider the local church a center of ministry to the community and the world. Although this expansion of interests is considered very desirable by the panel, the projection of its occurrence is based on somewhat conservative figures: 45 percent of the laity and over two-thirds of the clergy are projected to be interested in or knowledgeable about Christian actions and concerns on global societal issues by the year 2000.

Resources Needed by the Local Church

An important part of the shift in emphasis toward the local church's determination of its own activities began in the 1970s.

During that decade, the general boards and agencies of the denomination became financially unable to provide to the annual conferences and local churches as much resource material, direct consultation, and staff support as they had provided in the 1950s and 1960s. As less help was forthcoming from the general level of the denomination, more initiative was inspired on the local level to develop needed programs and resources.

Resource Persons Preferred Over Planned Programs. The Delphi study disclosed that local pastors and laity do not want the general agencies to initiate, develop, and forward to them programs which the local church is to implement. The 1978 survey of local church leadership confirmed this finding: The local church does not want to receive through the mail planned programs, particularly those for which they have not asked. There is a greater need for resource persons to be sent to the local church by the annual conference and general agency staffs to assist with programmatic needs and concerns being raised at the local level. Thus, the need is for the annual conference and general agencies to respond with appropriate resources rather than to develop new programs.

Growing Reliance on Annual Conference Agencies Rather Than on General Agencies. The Delphi panel sees the local church requesting more services and resources from annual conference agencies in the future, while predicting a slow but steady decline in the importance of the general agencies in providing resources to the local church. As the local church senses the general agencies' declining in importance, it will conclude that local concerns cannot or will not be dealt with effectively at the general level. The general agencies will retain their importance in providing guidance and resources to the annual conferences, with only a slight decline in importance of that role seen by the panel over the next two decades. Thus, it appears that when a local church faces a concern for which it

THE LOCAL CHURCH AND OTHER LEVELS

has not the needed resources, it will seek help at the closest point of contact: the annual conference staff.

The Need for Avenues of Communication Among Various Levels of Denomination. Part of the frustration of the local church with general agencies may result from an inability to communicate its needs effectively to the agencies and an apparent lack of responsiveness on the part of the general agencies. There is an urgent need for local chuches to have an avenue whereby their concerns and needs can be effectively registered with the general agencies.

The Delphi panel finds it very desirable for such avenues of communication to be opened to both the annual conference and general agencies. While there is little expectation among the panel that such avenues to the general agencies will be opened in the near future, more hope is expressed for effective communication lines to the general agencies by the year 2000. There is a great expectation that by 2000 there will have developed adequate methods of communication with annual conferences.

Analysis: More Frustration in Store? In light of the changing resourcing needs of the local church, The United Methodist Church must consider whether its various agencies will be able to answer adequately the requests expected to be made of them in the future.

We have noted the increasing need and desire of the local church to have agency staff persons come to the local scene for consultation and guidance. Yet such requests are being made at the very time when general agencies are being forced to reduce the number of field staff positions for economic reasons.

Futher, as the local church moves closer to home for program initiation and problem solution, the calls for assistance from the annual conference staffs will increase. A crisis may occur at the annual conference level if their personnel, financial, and other resources have not been increased to match the increased calls for assistance from local churches. In the absence of effective responses by annual conference staffs, local churches may develop toward the annual conference the same frustrations, tensions, and impressions of unresponsiveness presently felt toward the general agencies. The results of this frustration could lead to further internalization of focus by local churches and/or the seeking of resources from outside the denomination.

Local Church Organization

Localized Church Organization: Advantages and Disadvantages. Greater flexibility and freedom on the part of the local church to develop its own organizational pattern and style are predicted by the Delphi panel. Although some reservations were voiced, the majority of the panel approves of the continuation of this trend which has been observed during the past quadrennia. Increased flexibility of organizational patterns will facilitate the local church's handling of its own needs and concerns.

The panel also predicted, however, that in the long term, local church structures will tend not to reflect annual conference organizational patterns as closely as they do now. A majority feels this will be undesirable for the denomination. While individuality and creativity at the local level are valued, they could in the broader context create serious problems for the work of the annual conference, which needs some standardization among the local churches in order to serve them better. The difficulties of communicating with and providing resources for a large number of organizations are multiplied as standardization is reduced. Local churches and annual conferences will need to find effective methods of accommodation and viable working patterns if severe incongruence is not to develop. This will involve keeping open opportunities for creativity and problem-solving within the local chuch while at the same time maintaining continuity and compatibility with annual conference organizational programs and patterns.

Councils on Ministries: Increasing Importance. The local church Council on Ministries will be viewed increasingly as a viable organizational model by the year 2000, predicts the Delphi panel. They further predict that the district Councils on Ministries will become increasingly more important in the work of the annual conferences. These predictions seem to suggest that the concept of the Council on Ministries will be appreciated more fully and considered of increasing importance in future years.

A substantial majority of the panel sees the increasing importance of the local church and district Councils on Ministries as desirable for the denomination. These trends seem to suggest an enhanced ability of the local church and the district to plan and oversee programmatic work in the coming years. On many issues the locus of decision-making will move closer to the local church Council on Ministries than is presently the case. This will be true particularly if district councils develop into viable and purposeful organizations. As the locus for planning, coordination, resourcing, and carrying out the church's ministry moves in the direction of the local church, the immediacy of the tasks at hand may encourage local church members to become more involved.

Responsiveness and Accountability of Church Leadership: The Local Perspective

The United Methodist laity today is becoming increasingly vocal and assertive in requiring responsive and accountable leadership at all levels of the denomination. Members are eager to know that their expressed concerns are being heard at other levels of the denomination and that the support they give (time, personnel, financial) is being used wisely.

Ministerial Appointments. The Delphi panel forecast and almost unanimously found desirable an increasing intolerance by local church members of ministers who do not exhibit effective pastoral leadership. The laity is expected to become more aggressive in its demand for accountability in the appointive process in order to ensure the appointment of a local minister responsive to the needs of the local parish. Thus we may expect local church members to be increasingly unwilling to accept or retain clergy who have been ineffective in their pastoral ministry.

The Delphi panel overwhelmingly supported a proposed peer evaluation committee review of a minister's performance, to be conducted at the annual conference level. Yet the panel does not expect such a program of "ministers evaluating ministers" to be implemented.

If the projections are accurate, and no system of peer review is implemented, the laity's aggressive efforts to ensure a competent clergy may, by default, become *the* ministerial performance evaluation system. Thus, there is foreseeable in the next two decades open tension and conflict between the laity and the conference ministerial membership over ministerial performance evaluation and review.

Most of the trends seem to foreshadow strength among the laity at the local level as local members look more closely for accountability and responsiveness at the annual conference level. Indeed, the Delphi participants reached a strong consensus that the local church will not be more dominated by clergy than at present. The panel was almost unanimous in believing that this will work to the benefit of the denomination. Thus it appears that authority and power will move, if at all, in the direction of the laity of the local church.

Performance of Annual Conference and General Level Agencies. By 2000, the panel predicts, effective methods will have been established for evaluation of the performance of annual conference and general level agencies. This was called a favorable trend for The United Methodist Church, a way for the local membership to ensure that the other levels of the denomination are responsive to the needs of the local church, and that they are accountable for the use of the resources forwarded to them by the local church.

Summary. For many years primary emphasis within The United Methodist Church has been given to resourcing the programmatic needs of local churches on the basis of general and annual conference initiative, planning, and staffing. The Delphi panel predicts that priority attention in the years ahead will be given to issue and concerns arising in the local church. As more local churches are assessing their own specific ministry, resourcing, and maintenance needs and seeking the resources necessary to deal with these concerns, the movement is away from unquestioned support of general and annual conference programs and pronouncements. Local church members will have to be strongly convincing of the need and rationale for programs, activities, and institutions beyond the local church, and will be imposing more evaluation, responsiveness, and accountability requirements on the other levels of the denomination.

Two distinct possibilities exist as to how these trends will affect The United Methodist Church. The shift in focus to the local church may, on the one hand, result in a deepening of spiritual commitment to the task of the Christian church. The revitalization of individual congregations may be the leaven which restores vigor to the entire denomination. On the other hand, this shift of focus to the local church could, if wrongly conceived, be a major stimulus toward more congregational autonomy, thereby providing sufficient centrifugal force to begin the destruction of the polity and cohesiveness of the denomination.

Mutual understanding and support on the part of local churches and annual conference and general level ministries with regard to one another's concerns, needs, and programs are essential to the best interests of the denomination. The future of The United Methodist Church depends on whether we focus our continuing efforts, at least in part, on finding effective and viable ways to engender such mutual understanding and support of one another's concerns.

CHAPTER 5

Impact of Economic Issues

National and global economics dominate much of the thinking and planning of Americans. Details of economic trends and their causes have been reported in the first volume of this series.[1] Our purpose here is to examine the perceptions held by the lay and clergy Delphi project participants as to future economic trends and their effect on The United Methodist Church.

Inflation

Economic Effect on Denomination. The Delphi panel predicts that *inflation will continue to be a pervasive factor in our economy for many years.* Although expected to diminish by the year 2000, the rate of inflation is expected to continue at a relatively high level (6 to 10 percent or more) between now and 1984. The economic order in the near future is predicted to be unstable and very volatile, causing severe cycles of recession and growth. Although somewhat more stability is seen by the end of the century, the real income of the average family is expected to continue to decline for the next twenty years. Furthermore, health care costs are predicted to rise faster than personal income.

All of these economic forecasts are considered undesirable for The United Methodist Church. The individual's loss of purchasing power as a result of inflation will no doubt affect the economic setting of the local church and the denomination as a whole.

The 1978 survey of local church leaders disclosed that the problems precipitated by inflation are causing major economic concerns at the local church level. Difficulties experienced by the local church in meeting the congregational budget reflect an inability to raise enough funds to stay even with the cost of living and are consuming a large amount of time and thought at the local church level.

Effect on Policy Decisions. The impact of inflation is not only economic, but social and psychological as well. F. Thomas Juster, director of the Institute for Social Research at the University of Michigan, stated, "Virtually every piece of evidence we have indicates that consumers place inflation at the top of any list of serious economic and social problems—above unemployment, crime, war, racial strife, or urban decay."[2]

Major social impacts of inflation were discussed by Dr. Juster:

> One social cost is that inflation results in policy responses that slow down the economy, thus reducing real growth and creating unemployment. Consumers are very aware of this condition and it may play a large role in their negative reaction to inflation. Another real social cost may be the uncertainty that inflation creates for consumers and policy makers. Inflation and the expectation of future inflation clearly make it difficult to plan sensibly, to allocate resources to present and future needs in the appropriate amount, and in general to conduct one's financial affairs.[3]

The Delphi panel also seems to be pointing to the fact that inflation affects not only economic factors, but social and psychological matters as well. They point out not only that inflation will continue and that real income of families will lag behind the cost of living, but also that the impact of this situation on The United Methodist Church will be more than just economic. In the rest of this chapter we will discuss ways in

IMPACT OF ECONOMIC ISSUES

which economic issues will influence allocation of limited funds and policy decisions within the denomination.

Energy

Impact on the Denomination—Uncertainty. The problem of generating, in the face of inflation, sufficient income to maintain current levels of activity within the denomination is further complicated by the scarcity and high cost of energy.

The Delphi panel does not foresee the energy situation as being a stable one or beneficial to The United Methodist Church. A sharp increase in the cost of energy, particularly in the near future, is predicted. The panel further predicts that the United States government will not develop a viable energy-utilization policy in the next few years, that energy shortages will occur frequently during the next twenty years, and that viable alternatives to fossil fuels will not be adaptable for widespread use until the end of the century. Hence there will be no easy ways to alleviate shortages which occur or to make contingency plans for anticipated shortages.

This situation creates uncertainty for us not only as individuals, but also as persons planning and working together at all levels of The United Methodist Church. Our working environment in the future (even the ability to hold meetings at any level of the denomination) is difficult to anticipate as we face uncertain energy supplies. Energy-related problems place a new set of problems before The United Methodist Church, which must be addressed as we plan for the future: How will we assess the morality of the issues regarding consumption? How will we allocate financial resources in light of heightened need and demand? How can we help all parts of the denomination, including members, to handle the new set of circumstances?

Foreseeability of Problems: Need for Awareness. The energy problem is illustrative of the way in which anticipated facts, problems, and challenges can suddenly be thrust upon us from outside the denomination, forcing major transitions in the ways we utilize our resources and creating uncertainty as to whether we will even have some types of resources at all.

Was the energy crisis foreseeable ten years ago as we planned travel patterns and allocated financial resources? Could we have considered energy costs and conservation as we built and renovated facilities? In truth, the high cost and scarcity of fuel have been foreseen for several decades by those in fields related to energy resources.

What next will suddenly be thrust upon us, causing unanticipated changes in our outlook and working patterns? If we examine the literature of the specialists, the conversation is probably already there.

Taxation of Church Property

The Delphi panel predicts that as we move through the remainder of the century, more and more church-owned properties will be taxed. Although only a small portion of the panelists expect the church building itself to be taxed by the year 2000, most of the panel believes it likely that by the end of the century other properties of the church, such as parsonages and institutions, will be placed on the tax rolls. The negative economic impact of such taxation on local churches and other levels of the denomination would be enormous.

Keeping Pace with Inflation:
Slight Advantage Seen for Local Church

With inflation anticipated to continue at a high level, with personal real income expected to decline, and with energy costs rising sharply, the Delphi forecast is a predictable one: Neither the general church nor the annual conference nor the local churches will be able to keep pace with inflation, although some optimism is expressed for the local church in the long-term.

The local church, though expected to fall behind in real income in the near future, is given a somewhat better possibility of staying even with inflation by 2000. Over half the panel feel the local church has at least an even chance of keeping pace with inflation by the end of the century.

For the programs and activities at the general and annual conference levels, however, the long-term projection is a continuing decline in real income. An illustration in point deals with church-related colleges and universities. The panel feels that it is unlikely, especially by the year 2000, that church-related institutions of higher learning will be able to compete financially with government-supported colleges and universities. Considerable resources will be needed from private sources, including the denomination. While it is considered highly desirable to support these institutions, the Delphi panel predicts that the resources simply will not be available for the denomination to support United Methodist-related colleges and universities at a level which will enable them to weather the twin problems of increased costs and smaller enrollments.

Thus, the impact of inflation will be most severe at the levels beyond the local church.

Response of the Local Church to Economic Issues

Retention of Funds at Local Level. In view of the increasing tendency of the local church to focus inward and the continuously diminishing purchasing power, one may expect local churches to retain more of their resources in the future to meet their own needs before underwriting programs at other levels of the denomination.

Indeed the 1978 survey of local church leadership disclosed that the funds available for programs and benevolences at the local level and at other levels of the denomination are severely limited by the increased cost of maintaining local church property and supporting those employed at the local level.

Dr. Robert L. Wilson of the Divinity School of Duke

University found in a recent study that between 1967 and 1976 changes did occur in the way funds were expanded by local United Methodist churches.[4] In 1976, local churches were spending more of their funds maintaining their own programs than in ministries beyond the local church. The shifts in spending patterns were caused by (1) decreased purchasing power of the churches (inflation more than offset the fact that giving increased during this period) and (2) new demands placed on the local congregation. For example, at the end of the ten-year study, a larger proportion of local church funds was going for current expenses, minister's salary, and other ministerial support items, particularly pension and health benefits, while a smaller portion was used for debt retirement, building improvements, connectional funds, and benevolences.

Economic pressures are creating tension within the local church. At the same time that the local churches are facing a need to retain more of their resources at home because of inflation and the rapidly changing economic environment, they are receiving more and more calls for financial help from annual conference and general-level institutions and agencies. The way a local church views and deals with its financial problems will largely determine not only how it fulfills its ministry, but also the extent to which it feels willing and able to support benevolence activities beyond the local church.

Negative Attitude Toward Funding Programs Beyond the Local Level. The local church attitude toward requests for funding of programs beyond the local level was the topic of several predictions by the Delphi panel. The panel predicted that the local church laity will become more resistant to askings and apportionments from both the annual conference and general-church levels. Programs beyond the local church will be viewed increasingly as a burden and a drain on local church resources that could better be used at home. Accordingly, less monies will be forwarded to programs and causes beyond the local church, and much that is sent will be designated for specific projects.

The resistance to askings and apportionments by agencies beyond the local church is seen as undesirable for the denomination. With regard to the general-level askings and apportionments, resistance is seen throughout the next two decades. Similar resistance directed toward the annual conference, however, is seen as limited in 1984, but increasing by 2000. This seems to correlate with other trends predicted by the Delphi panel, i.e., increasing demands on annual conference agencies in the near term, reflecting the move away from general-level activities toward local and annual conference concerns. As the annual conference agencies find more demands being placed on them by local churches, they may have difficulty responding adequately, particularly in the face of growing economic pressures. If adequate responses are not forthcoming from annual conferences, the local churches will be less willing to participate in conference programs, particularly financially burdensome ones.

The view of programs beyond the local church as a burden and drain on local church resources, or indeed even as a threat to the existence of the local parish, is considered undesirable by the Delphi panel. So, too, is the prediction that local churches will forward fewer resources to programs and causes at other levels of the denomination.

Predictions of future local church response to requests for funding and support of programs beyond the local church seem to correlate well with materials presented in the preceding chapter. Economic problems will augment the increased focus on the local church. Priorities must be established to deal with the many demands placed on increasingly limited financial resources. As priorities are focused in the local church, work at other levels of the denomination will suffer.

Designation of Projects to Receive Monies Forwarded by Local Church. The panel was almost equally divided as to the desirability of the projection that local churches will specifically designate projects to receive a large portion of the funds they forward. The lack of consensus probably indicates that considerable discussion will center around this issue in years to come.

Part of the discussion of designated giving will center around the extent to which the local church benefits from work done by the general and annual conference agencies. To the extent that agency programs and projects facilitate the meeting of local needs *as seen by the local church,* they may receive support from the local congregation. Thus, the local church will be holding the general and annual conference agencies accountable not only for their use of resources, but also for their function in helping to meet the needs of the local congregation *as that congregation views those needs.* The question will be: Who decides which projects and programs are worthy of continuing support—the agencies or the local churches?

Summary. Trends foreseen in the local churches run counter to what the panel members believe desirable for The United Methodist Church. The local laity will have to be more firmly convinced in the future of the need and logic of programs, institutions, and activities beyond the local church level before it will invest its limited funds in these programs. The shift will be away from the unquestioned support of the general and annual conference agencies, programs, and pronouncements and toward the work of the local church.

CHAPTER 6

Expectations of and for Leadership

The task of leadership within The United Methodist Church is becoming more complex. Conflict is unavoidable when a community of people seeks to work together for a common purpose while at the same time striving to meet individual interests and needs. Differences inevitably occur over priorities. Within the denomination requests of frequently conflicting groups complicate the development and administration of policies. Furthermore, our productivity and effectiveness are being increasingly influenced by factors outside the denomination, such as inflation and energy. Nevertheless there is an urgent call for leadership and guidance in moral, spiritual, and policy matters.

Problems of leadership are not unique to The United Methodist Church. A real or presumed remoteness and lack of responsiveness cause leaders of most large organizations today to face conflict with constituents who want to be more influential in administrative and organizational decisions.

"The greatest problem facing today's institutions," says Warren Bennis, "is *the concatenation of external forces that impinge and impose upon it events outside the skin boundary of the organization.*"[1] Bennis isolates two of these forces which he labels key factors leading to the decline of confidence in and respect for today's leaders:

1) a new populism in the nation, marked by a clamor for authority by a broad base of people not in leadership, and

2) a polarization of attitudes concerning basic values. In Bennis's words, *"Within the community, we have not only a loss of*

consensus over basic values, we have as well a polarization. We have not a consensus but a dissensus."[2]

Creative leadership is crucial to the productivity and effectiveness of any organization. But the organization must be able to develop and support this leadership. In this chapter we will examine some predictions concerning several leadership offices and functions within The United Methodist Church.

United Methodist Bishops

Changes in leadership patterns occurring in society are illustrated in the role of United Methodist bishops. There have been some formal changes, consisting of modifications in the rights, duties, powers, and authority of individual bishops. Other changes have been informal, resulting from differing styles of individual bishops, altered circumstances in the annual conferences, and differing expectations placed on the office of bishop by clergy and laity.

As to the future role of bishops, the Delphi panel predicts the following trends:

1) Limitation of the tenure of bishops to twelve years is likely to occur by the end of the century, though not in the near future. The advisability of limiting the tenure of bishops was vigorously debated by the 1976 General Conference, but the historic denominational pattern of life tenure of bishops, i.e., to age of retirement, was retained. The Delphi panel apparently believes that the issue, having been thoroughly discussed in 1976, will not continue to be an issue for debate in the near future. However, the panel predicts that limited tenure for bishops is likely to be realized by the year 2000, with over half the panelists indicating that this change would be desirable for the denomination.

2) The office of bishop will retain its importance in the governance of the denomination in the near future. While no clear consensus as to the importance of bishops was found in the predictions for the year 2000, a decline in their importance

is considered somewhat more probable by then than by 1984. The panel considers very undesirable a diminished role for bishops in the long-term future.

3) A collegial style of administration (defined as sharing openly in discussion and decision-making with the laity and clergy) is not very likely to be developed by individual bishops by 1984, but there is a strong projection for greater collegiality in administration by the end of the century. This forecast is probably based on the panelists' realization that administrative style is highly dependent on a bishop's background and personality, and that the collegial model of administration has only recently had widespread discussion and acceptance. Since many of the present bishops do not employ a collegial style of administration, a shift in this direction will not occur until others are elected to the episcopacy who have incorporated the collegial model into their personal working styles.

4) The Council of Bishops will enjoy no increase of influence on policy determination within the denomination in the years ahead. No consensus emerged as to the desirability of this forecast regarding the council, which has historically been given the general role of overseeing the church in spiritual and temporal matters.

These projections by the Delphi panel indicate that while the bishops will continue to be held in respect within the denomination, they are not expected to exercise more influence on policy matters. The panel was uncertain as to whether this will benefit the denomination. It is unclear whether the forecast results from the apparent tide running against strong leadership, either individually or collectively, or from the panel's inability to see any great strength of leadership in the council.

District Superintendents

In various studies of the office of the district superintendent during the past two decades, differing views have surfaced as to the role and function of the district superintendent. Laity, clergy, and the district superintendents themselves have frequently held different views as to the most important functions of the office. Considerable differences have been revealed between what are considered to be the most important functions of the district superintendent and what consumes the largest amount of their time. Perceptions differ as to what is needed and how time is spent. For example, the 1978 study showed that laity, clergy, and superintendents all agreed that the *most important function* of the district superintendent (of a list of eighteen functions) is the *training of pastors to serve and resource their laity.*[3] While this function is valued more highly than administrative tasks which consume the time and energy of superintendents, it ranked ninth in terms of the amount of time devoted to it. By contrast, laity, clergy, superintendents, and bishops agreed that one of the least important functions of the district superintendent in forwarding the mission of the church is serving on annual conference boards and agencies. Yet this administration task ranked fifth among activities consuming the time of the district superintendent.

None of the Delphi panel's predictions for the future of the office of the district superintendent are considered desirable for The United Methodist Church. They predict that:

1) The laity will increasingly view the district superintendent more as district managers with administrative tasks and less as presiding elders with religious and symbolic functions.

2) The district superintendency will begin to decline in importance in governing the annual conferences in the latter years of this century, though not in the immediate future.

3) The importance of the district superintendency in the leadership of the local church will remain essentially constant during the next two decades, with only a very modest increase in role forecast for the year 2000. While a majority of the panel

believes it to be in the best interests of the denomination for the district superintendents to be more influential in the local church, it appears that as they become more occupied with administrative and organizational needs at levels beyond the local church, their impact on the local congregations will not grow significantly.

Call for Evaluation and Accountability

In chapter 4 we noted projections relating to the increased demand for evaluation and accountability of leaders of the denomination. These demands will be made not only of ministers and denominational agencies, but of bishops and district superintendents as well.

Lay Evaluation of Individual Leaders' Performance. As the laity begin to assess more closely the competence and effectiveness of their pastoral leadership, they will discover that the pastor's authority stems not from the position itself, but from the skills of the individual holding the position. This understanding will lead to more careful evaluation of the performance of the individual pastor.

As the same understandings develop with regard to the performance of agency administrators, district superintendents, and bishops, more evaluation mechanisms will be instituted. Already in existence are first efforts for evaluating bishops and district superintendents. The 1976 General Conference established the annual conference Committee on Episcopacy and the annual conference Committee on the District Superintendency (paragraphs 733 and 758, respectively, 1976 *Book of Discipline*).

Peer Evaluation. Higher standards of ministerial performance will be required by the clergy as well as the laity. Peer evaluation of ministers is beginning in several conferences and is likely to become more common as a result of a combination of factors.

Ministers want to be evaluated as individual professionals, and not simply as members of a collective group of clergy. They seek greater opportunity for advancement, greater control over the work setting, and greater remuneration on the basis of their individual performance. As the view of the annual conference shifts from that of a "brotherhood" of persons engaged in a joint mission to that of an association of essentially self-employed professionals, both clergy and laity will be less tolerant of the incompetent pastor. Thus, adequacy of performance must be evaluated to facilitate the determination of advancement, remuneration, and, in case of an oversupply of clergy, disqualification from the profession.

Accountability. In addition to evaluation of their individual performance and effectiveness, leaders of the church will be subject to *a critical assessment of their actions.* Not just individual leaders will be held accountable for their actions, however. As economic pressures mount and emphasis shifts to the local level, the laity will seek an increasingly influential voice in decisions and will expect and demand more responsiveness from institutions and agencies beyond the local church. Policies developed and implemented by general and conference-level agencies will be subject to a more critical assessment. Thus can be seen a movement away from a blind acceptance by constituents of the actions of officials toward a more critical assessment of their actions.

The cause of increased demand for official accountability is constitutents' disagreement with or lack of information about the rationales behind administrative decisions and actions. When the bases of decisions made by leadership are not understood or shared by constituents, resulting actions often appear to be in conflict with the best interests and desires of constituents. The intent of those calling for evaluation and accountability, then, is not to destroy the integrity and purpose of leadership, but rather to produce official responsiveness to the needs of constituents and to facilitate constituents' understanding of and participation in decisions which determine the actions of that leadership.

A Call to Leadership

While the Delphi participants disclose an increasing desire for evaluation of and accountability by leaders at every level of the denomination, the study also indicates that the denomination is not turning away from the leadership of bishops, district superintendents, and pastors. Questions being raised about these officials are not in terms of acceptance or nonacceptance of the leadership positions themselves, but in terms of the performance of persons holding the positions—matters of competence, accountability, and responsiveness to and awareness of the work of the local churches. As resources become more scarce and the desire grows at the local level for a greater voice in decision-making processes, leaders beyond the local church will have to become more sensitive to the needs and concerns of the local church, more open and communicative concerning the rationales behind their administrative policy decisions, and more precise in their actions. Leaders, who find this type of work environment uncomfortable, whether they be bishops, district superintendents, pastors, or administrators, will increasingly be at odds with their constituencies. Those who can readily share and discuss with their constituents information and rationales behind their administrative decisions will be more comfortable and effective in the work environment of the future.

The challenge at every level of The United Methodist Church is to find strong, creative, and sensitive leadership, who will find in The United Methodist Church a constituency ready and willing to support its efforts. The alternative is best described by Warren Bennis:

> *It is the paradox of our time that precisely when the trust and credibilities of leaders are at their lowest, when the beleaguered survivors in leadership*

positions feel unable to summon up the vestige of power left to them, we most need people who can lead. The alternative, it seems to me, is a heightening of our present danger, an increase in the sort of organizational paralysis that is already endemic in our institutions, a failure of nerve that could pave the way for a new and perhaps more insidious type of demigod.[4]

CHAPTER 7

Organizational Issues Before the Denomination

Every organization, large or small, must develop patterns and policies for instructing and regulating its members. Basic doctrines and pronouncements form the basis for customs and traditions, rules and regulations, which develop with the passage of time.

So it has been with The United Methodist Church. Methodism was established in this country in 1784 under the direct guidance of John Wesley through his "superintendents," Thomas Coke and Francis Asbury. Guiding principles were those developed by Wesley for the governing of Methodist societies in England. The first departure from the instructions of John Wesley occurred at the 1784 Christmas Conference in Baltimore where the process of defining the unique rules and regulations of Methodism in the United States was begun. Through the years, customs, traditions, policies, and laws for governing the denomination have been enlarged, revised, and codified in *The Book of Discipline*. In addition, there are annual conferences rules of order and policy statements, general agency and institution by-laws, constitutions, articles of incorporation, and policy actions.

Today it is difficult to appreciate and understand all the factors which have culminated in the present organizational structure of The United Methodist Church. Nor is it always readily apparent how and why the denomination functions as it does today. Current interpretations of several aspects of the governing procedures have caused misgivings to be voiced within the denomination. Some of these organizational issues will be examined in this chapter.

The Development of Policy and Direction

General Conference. Broad legislative guidelines for The United Methodist Church have traditionally been established by the General Conference, whose authority is derived from the constitution but also from powers granted to it by the annual conferences.

The Delphi panel predicted that the General Conference will continue to serve as a viable means of establishing legislation for the denomination, and most panel members believe it is desirable for the General Conference to fulfill this function.

The panel also considers it desirable for the General Conference to serve as the instrumentality for developing purposes and goals for the denomination. However, the panel *predicts that by 1984 the General Conference will not be able to provide the denomination with clear purposes, goals, and directions.* No consensus developed as to the ability of the General Conference to serve in this capacity in the year 2000.

Annual Conferences. The Delphi panel predicts that by 2000 more control and legislative direction will originate at the annual conference level than at the General Conference level. Only 20 percent of the panel considered this an undesirable trend, and no consensus developed regarding its occurrence by 1984.

General Agencies. A slight majority of the panel considers it desirable for the general agencies to play a more important role in the development of goals and directions for the denomination than they do today. Yet the panel was almost equally divided as to the probability of such a trend during the next two decades.

Challenge: Optimum Utilization of Denominational Structure for Development of Policy and Direction. There is a high level of confidence in the work of the General Conference. It serves well in its legislative role. In recent years, however, dissatisfaction has developed over the extraordinarily crowded agenda imposed on members of the quadrennial General Conference. Furthermore, many issues raised in our rapidly changing society, and changing social, economic, and missional issues within the denomination, demand quick responses which cannot be met by a body which meets only once every four years. As the number of petitions for legislative action increases, as the range of issues for debate grows larger, and as the economic ramifications of such large meetings change, we must closely monitor the functioning of the General Conference so that we may discover at the earliest possible time which activities are becoming dysfunctional and what unrealistic expectations are being placed on the General Conference.

Appropriate alternative means may need to be found at other points in the organizational structure of the denomination to handle functions and activities which now fill the agenda of the General Conference but have become inappropriate to or outside the ability of the General Conference to handle. The Delphi panel has pointed out that in the long term annual conferences are expected to be more viable for legislative development. Certainly the yearly meeting schedule of the annual conferences provides more flexibility in program development, budgets, and policy adjustments than is provided by the quadrennial schedule of the General Conference.

A specific issue needing attention was exposed by the Delphi study. Doubt was expressed that the General Conference will be able to provide clear purposes, goals, and directions for the denomination in the near future. Perhaps this group of knowledgeable United Methodists is suggesting that the type of reflection necessary for formulating basic goals, purposes, and directions cannot be scheduled during quadrennial two-week working sessions of the General Conference. If this task is no longer appropriate to or within the ability of the General Conference to handle, where will this be done? The role of the general agencies in this task is unclear, and there is no strong expectation that the Council of Bishops can fulfill this function. If conceptualization of basic purpose and direction is being accomplished at the local church level, how may we build the strength of consensus to inform and guide the entire denomination? We must discover at what point in our organizational structure the necessary reflection is taking place for the development of basic purposes and goals for The United Methodist Church, or, if no such reflection is presently in progress, we must find the most appropriate place in our organization to undertake this task.

The challenge to the denomination is to realize optimum utilization of existing denominational structure for the most effective governing of the denomination.

Issues Relating to the Professional Ministry

Evolving Self-Interest. Alexis De Toqueville analyzed with precision the character and nature of American society as he viewed it in 1835.

> No novelty in the United States struck me more vividly during my stay there than the equality of conditions.
> I soon realized that the influence of this fact extends far beyond political mores and laws, exercising dominion over civil society as much as over government; it creates opinions, gives birth to feelings, suggests customs, and modifies whatever it does not create.
> So the more I studied American society, the more clearly I saw equality of conditions as the creative elements from which each particular fact derived, and all my observations constantly returned to this nodal point.[1]

In its earliest days the annual conference of The United Methodist Church, viewed as the professional association of clergy, operated under the principle of equality of conditions—equality in appointment, service, remuneration, and status. Through the years differentiation developed in tasks, scale of responsibilities, and salary. But still, as De Toqueville observed in American society as a whole, there prevailed within the professional ministry the influence of and belief in the general principle of equality of conditions. Until the last two decades the annual conference, serving as the association of professional peers, was the primary forum for interaction among the clergy. It was recognized, of course, that neither appointments nor salaries were equal, but it was still presumed that opportunities were equal. Indeed, as one proceeded through one's career, a pattern of advancement developed embracing greater responsibilities and larger salaries. The final remuneration, pension compensation, was and is today based on years of service rather than on measure of responsibility undertaken (fulfilled) or salary received.

Today, however, as ministers submit to increasingly critical evaluation by both laity and clergy (see chapter 6) and as they realize the "brotherhood" concept of equality of opportunity (if not actual assignment) is no longer a viable principle in the profession, they are beginning to seek appointments, advancement, "entitlements," and rewards on the basis of individual performance rather than on the basis of how they fit into a conference-wide appointment scheme. There is developing, to use Daniel Bell's phrase concerning the total society, a revolution of rising entitlement.[2] In addition to increased compensation, ministers are seeking more determination in appointments, more control over personal life-styles (typified by the current debate over pastor-owned versus church-owned parsonages), and travel, utility, and educational allowances.

Thus, significant changes are occurring in the way the pastor's profession is viewed by both laity and clergy. Expectations are changing with regard to evaluation of a minister's performance by the local laity, by the district superintendent, and by the bishop. As there grows among local laity the practice of evaluating pastoral performance and effectiveness and compensating ministers according to individual merit, we may foresee considerable dissatisfaction with present methods of making ministerial appointments and setting ministerial compensation. Some of these issues were reviewed by the Delphi panel.

Salary and Related Benefits. Rising expectations for economic support of the professional ministry by the denomination can be seen in pressures to underwrite not only increased salaries, but also pension, health, and other benefit programs which are salary-related. In addition to the cost of funding previously incurred pension obligations, pressure exists to increase current pension benefits. Indeed, the largest items in many annual conference budgets today are related to ministerial support—pension plans, health and other insurance, district superintendents' funds, and minimum salary programs.

A large majority of the Delphi panel forecasts that in the coming years a major portion of time and energies of the annual conferences will be spent dealing with economic issues affecting the professional ministry. Furthermore, the panel members consider it appropriate for the annual conference to handle these matters.

The panel foresees a reasonable likelihood, however, that rising expectations by the clergy for economic support will produce significant tensions between laity and clergy. Eighty percent of the panel foresee at least an even chance that by 1984 increased salary expectations by the clergy will produce significant tensions between laity and clergy at the annual conference level. While half of the panel sees only an even chance that such tension will develop by 2000, a full 35 percent expect significant tensions to develop within the annual conference by the year 2000. This is seen as an unfortunate development. It is interesting to note, further, that the panel expects less of this kind of tension to develop at the local church level than within the annual conference as a whole. The panel was almost equally divided as to whether increased salary expectations by the clergy would produce tensions between clergy and laity at the local church level by 1984. There is some shifting of opinion toward its likelihood by 2000, but it is not a strong or marked change.

One reason for this difference may be found in the data discussed in chapter 5 dealing with the expectation that the local church will be better able to cope with inflation than will the annual conference or general levels of the denomination. Perhaps in this instance the panel believes that the local church will be able to handle requests for increased ministerial remuneration at the local level, but will not be able to respond to the collective requirements and requests of the annual conference portion of the ministerial support system.

Guaranteed Appointment System Under Authority of Bishop. The system of ministerial assignment to local churches under the direction of the bishop has been one of the fundamental polity principles of The United Methodist Church. In exchange for being guaranteed a position, a pastor accepts the obligation to serve the congregation to which he is appointed. However, today the right of the bishop to make ministerial assignments and the pastor's guaranteed appointment are being discussed with increasing frequency.

Over half of the Delphi panel believes there is at least an even chance that by 1984 the guaranteed ministerial appointment system, under the authority of the bishop, will be modified or eliminated. A slightly stronger prediction is made for modification of the system by the year 2000. Half the panel considers this undesirable for The United Methodist Church.

Pastoral Challenge of Authority. The Delphi panel expects that in the years ahead pastors as a group will, more strongly than today, challenge existing polity provisions relating to the clergy, such as the appointment process, itinerancy, and the authority of bishops and district superintendents. A majority of the panel considers this an undesirable trend for The United Methodist Church, but the likelihood of such a challenge of authority appears to be great for 1984 and even greater for the year 2000.

Thus rises the challenge to many of the present policies and practices of The United Methodist Church. The way in which the denomination is able to resolve some of these basic issues focusing on the professional ministry will in large measure determine the future course of much of the governing polity of the denomination. The Delphi study indicates that some of the foreseeable trends run counter to what is considered best for the denomination. These important issues must be given careful consideration in order for the denomination to determine policies which are best suited to its future life and work.

Diversity and Unity in Christ

Diversity is part of the heritage of The United Methodist Church. The denomination has traditionally welcomed into its membership persons of differing occupations, social classes, educational levels, and racial, ethnic, and national heritages. The Delphi panel foresees that The United Methodist Church will experience, during the next two decades, a gradually increasing diversity of both theological perspectives and membership. Furthermore, the panel expects that the denomination will continue to affirm the distinctiveness of racial and ethnic groups within the denomination rather than seeking an amalgamation and integration of these groups with the majority. These predictions are seen by the panel as desirable for The United Methodist Church.

The related organizational issue deals with how we will allow increased diversity to affect our unity. Will we focus on specific interests of limited groups, emphasizing those matters which separate, and fail to find that subtle balance between individual and group needs? Only to the extent that we understand, appreciate, and share the unifying mission of our Christian heritage can we celebrate our diversity. Would that we might rejoice in the uniqueness of differing interests, viewpoints, backgrounds, and abilities to fulfill our joint task in the context of our heritage as United Methodists.

CHAPTER 8

Criteria for Assessing Future Directions

The informed leadership of the denomination who participated in the Delphi project considered many predicted trends undesirable for the future of The United Methodist Church. Perhaps one of the most disconcerting facts disclosed by the project is the unwillingness of the denomination as a whole to assess its future.

Policy Development: The Need for Leadership

The highest level of consensus on any of the 122 statements presented to the Delphi panel appeared regarding the *need for The United Methodist Church to develop a clear sense of purpose and identity for its life and work.* But expectations of the panel regarding this highly desirable goal are not optimistic.

The same issue disclosed a very high level of consensus among local church pastors, lay leadership, and annual conference directors participating in the 1978 survey. They termed the *need for the denomination to rediscover a sense of purpose and identity* one of the most pressing issues before the denomination between now and 1984. They expressed a further need for *leadership in this reassessment of direction* for the church.

A factor contributing to our failure to sense our own identity and destiny is the social environment of our nation. Significant changes, major tensions, and increasing divergencies within our society seem to focus on those things which make us different—different from the past, different from each other, different in perspective, and different in needs. Within the denomination various groups are seeking individual identity, a phenomenon recently called "the growing tribalism of United Methodism."[1]

A lack of purpose was noted in society as a whole by Thomas Griffith. Reflecting on the bicentennial of the United States, he wrote, "The original goals have mostly been realized. The new ones haven't been agreed upon."[2] He described an educated, articulate, and concerned populace possessing many skills and talents which are not being focused.

> The result is not a society gone soft, unpatriotic, or indifferent, but thwarted and baffled. Its members may feel powerless to achieve but can be quite forceful in denying, and they now demand, in a thousand little forays, that all institutions—government and business, particularly—pay them heed. They do so in an often sour spirit of scorning, piecemeal victories over what they cannot on the whole change.[3]

Read these words again, substituting for society "The United Methodist Church"—local, annual conference, and/or general levels. The description fits remarkably well. The reasons? *Lack of direction* for the denomination and *lack of leadership* to articulate the steps for moving forward.

Who will guide the development of policy and direction for the denomination? The Delphi panel does not expect the General Conference, the Council of Bishops, or the general agencies to provide the leadership needed to articulate denominational purposes and policies. Who will do this? There is no central forum for hearing common concerns and facilitating necessary decision-making. Mechanisms have not been established to build a consensus among local churches or annual conferences so that agreement on overall denominational purposes and directions can be reached and necessary policies establishd for action.

Instead, many groups and special interests have articulated their positions and are seeking to win adherents to their point of view. Few voices are speaking to the *total perspective* of the denomination. If there is no understanding of policy and direction for the denomination as a whole, the value and worth of individual group perspectives cannot be adequately or validly assessed and policy-making becomes policy by politics rather than policy by purpose.

One of the major tasks before the denomination, then, is to develop a means and/or group to guide, from the perspective of the entire denomination, the conceptualization of policy for the entire denomination.

Accountability: The Call for Effective Performance and Multi-level Participation in Administrative Decisions

The growing demand for evaluation and accountability has been noted earlier (see chapter 4). Two reasons are seen for this attitude. First there is the demand for effective performance at all levels of the denomination. As local churches demand effective performance by annual conference and general agencies, we see a reversal of the practice of general and annual conference-level evaluation of the performance of local churches. The concern is to see that those in positions of responsibility exercise their authority with economy and efficiency. But monitoring activities and programs to see that they are properly conceived and administered is not the only concern.

Accountability is demanded also because laity and clergy want a better understanding of the rationales underlying decisions which affect the denomination and want to be involved in decisions made on their behalf. Conflict has arisen over this issue because under the present system laity and clergy do not know what policies are being administered, have not participated in the formulation of these policies, and therefore do not understand or have ownership in the actions which are being taken. Persons at all levels want to participate in the formation of policies which determine administrative action. Thus, we see that if denominational policies are to be effective in carrying forward the desired mission, programs, and activities, those policies must be clearly stated and largely agreed upon.

Policies—The Criteria for Judgment

It is very difficult for an organization as large and diverse as The United Methodist Church to articulate a sharp, clear statement of its purpose and goal. It is particularly difficult in an organization in which decision-making is so diffuse and membership is voluntary. Yet some sense of collective will is needed in order to make important decisions affecting the future: How are we to deal with pessimistic predictions for the future? On what basis are decisions to be made? How shall we allocate our resources?

The key task in the development of purpose and direction does not lie in the formulation of the statement itself. It lies in the development of *policies* or *criteria for judgment*. In order to accomplish its purposes, the denomination must make appropriate judgments about allocation of resources. Judgments made only because of immediate expediency will not satisfy the long-term needs of the denomination. Judgments made without adequate rationale will not satisfy the increasing calls for accountability. We must first develop appropriate criteria for judgment, or policies.

John Scharr made a helpful description of the search for a meaningful future. He wrote:

> The future is not a result of choices among alternative paths offered by the present, but a place that is created—created first in the mind and will, created next in activity. The future is not some place we are going to, but one we are creating. The paths to it are not found but made, and the activity of making them changes both the maker and the destination.[4]

He advises us not simply to observe which choices are available. He advises us to create our choices from the collective reflections of the mind and the determination of the will, and thus develop our future. With such a future in mind, policies can be developed and articulated—policies which will become criteria for evaluation and accountability and for judging decisions relating to the allocation of time, personnel, and financial resources. Without such criteria for judgment, the adequacy of decisions being made cannot be properly evaluated. Policies, the criteria for judgment, must be established if the denomination is to formulate a clear statement of its purpose and move into the future with resolve.

CHAPTER 9

Images of the Future

The Delphi study has helped us to visualize the future of The United Methodist Church. By assessing future trends we gain information and a valuable new perspective from which to explore our future goals and mandates in the name of Christ.

Yet the complex and changing nature of today's society, both technologically and socially, seems to resist a considered analysis of the impact of the future on us, both individually and collectively. Often we are overwhelmed by the crises and disorganization which seem unique to our time. "Not in the lifetime of most men has there been so much grave and deep apprehension.... The domestic economic situation is in chaos. Our dollar is weak throughout the world. Prices are so high as to be utterly impossible. Of our troubles man can see no end." The quotation fits today, but was written in *Harpers Weekly* in 1857 to describe American society.

Some feel that the environment today is more complex than in the past, that the United States and many of its institutions are undergoing a major period of transition which began in the 1960s and will continue until the end of the century. This statement, written in 1969, may accurately describe our present situation, both in the nation and in the denomination:

> The problems of transition are being compounded by a number of complex considerations: (1) the rate of change which is shrinking research and planning time; (2) outdated criteria used to examine new problems and opportunities; (3) micro and piecemeal ways of dealing with problems of macro scale; (4) public insistence on "instant" solutions and leader impatience with problems that

demand attention over longer periods of time; (5) inexperience in bringing about large-scale collaboration on the part of leaders in and between private and public sectors; (6) the pushing and pulling on the part of those who, through fear or selfish interests, resist change, and those who want to lead and accelerate it; (7) competing demands for scarce talents and resources and increasingly frequent absence of needed skills; (8) uncertainty on the part of decision makers and institutions as to the nature of their new roles and responsibilities in a changing society; (9) the temporary inability of our system of checks and balances, of regulations and controls, to function effectively during the transition; and (10) the question of how to regularize the irregular.[1]

Ours *is* a time of transition. We are reminded in Hebrews 13:14, "For here we have no lasting city, but we seek the city which is to come." Thus must our denomination look to the future. Fred Polak tells us that Christianity in the western world has lost its vision, its sense of eschatology,* and the ability to provide strength for tomorrow. He urges the revival of an "image of the future" with its glorious possibilities and promises. In his words,

> The image of the future can act not only as barometer, but as a regulative mechanism which alternatively opens and shuts the dampers on the mighty blast-furnace of culture. It not only indicates alternative choices and possibilities, but actively promotes certain choices and in effect puts them to work in determining the future. A close examination of prevailing images, then, puts us in a position to forecast the probable future.
>
> Any culture which finds itself in the condition of our present culture, turning aside from its own heritage of positive visions of the future, or actively at work in changing these positive values into negative ones, has no future unless strong counterforces are set in motion soon. This view is of crucial importance for practical policy. It opens up new vistas for policy-makers in the areas where they will have freedom of planning and action.[2]

*The beliefs about the end of life in this world and the view of the last things such as the return of Christ, the resurrection, judgment, and the New Age.

As Christians we prepare for the future so that Christ's message can be presented to those living in the future. United Methodism has its unique task in this larger enterprise, but in order to move forward with purpose and commitment, *we must deal constructively with fundamental issues and trends of the future.* We must develop policy and plan actions so that The United Methodist Church can influence in the name of Christ the future course of God's world.

The Task of Each United Methodist

How do we begin to establish guidelines for our denomination as it moves into the future? We begin first as individuals, committed to Christ and the earthly ministry of his church. Each of us is called to study and reflect on the nature of his teachings and their relevance to ourselves and to the local church, community, nation, and world. As we mature in our understanding of how the kingdom is to be manifested in this world, our individual potential and responsibilities become more clear to us. When we join other Christians as United Methodists, our study and reflection move into a group context. Through joint study and reflection, we strive for a level of Christian maturity which will enable us to develop a mutually shared understanding of our joint mission in the local parish. In this way we establish goals and policies for our local congregation. Whether we engage directly in this process or entrust the task of reflection to others, we must then rely on someone to implement the policies on which we have reached a consensus—someone to guide us as we carry out our work.

This process applies to every task we face within the denomination. Our need today is to reexamine the mission of our Christian community, The United Methodist Chuch. It requires a willingness to register our convictions openly, to develop trust in responsible leadership, and to encourage and support the consensus developed in our decision-making (legislative) bodies.

We are not called to participate in an elaborate or complex technology of determining our future, but rather to develop a vision, *an image of the future we intend for our denomination.* We are called to discover those who can help us to formulate appropriate policies, criteria by which to make our decisions. We are called to find, trust, and support those who can lead us in putting these policies into action. And finally, we are called to hold both our leaders and ourselves accountable for the actions of our denomination.

In this reflective search, strength will come not primarily from the bishops, the general agencies, the annual conferences, or even the General Conference, although meetings of these groups will be enlightened and enriched by contributions from many sources. The unique power at the heart of United Methodism has always been involvement of a concerned laity and clergy at the local level. In this search for clarity of goal and for leadership, God's strength will be manifested primarily as individuals committed to Christ share their mature reflection of Christ's teachings in group conversation, discussion, and prayer.

As the prayerful conversation and discussion continue, the projections presented in this book should be used to illumine, not determine, the image of the future of The United Methodist Church. These projections can inform, stimulate, and challenge the reader to reflect on the issues presented, so that we may rediscover why we gather under the banner of United Methodism. Together, we shall explore and develop goals, policies, and criteria for evaluating actions, so that as we enter our third century, The United Methodist Church will be a part of God's glorious plan for the future.

Appendix A

The Delphi technique has been well described in the context of its use by an industrial group.

> The basic characteristics of the Delphi [technique] are (1) anonymity, (2) iteration with controlled feedback, (3) statistical group responses. Anonymity is achieved by using questionnaires, where specific responses are not associated with individual members of the group. This is a way of cutting down on the effect of dominant individuals and reducing group pressure. Iteration consists in performing the interaction among members of the group in several stages; typically, at the beginning of each stage the results of the previous stage are summarized and fed back to members of the group, and they are then asked to reassess their answers in the light of what the entire group thought on the previous round. Finally, rather than asking the group to arrive at a consensus, the group opinion is taken to be a statistical average of the final opinion of individual members. The opinion of every member is reflected in the group response.
>
> The net result of a Delphi experience is a convergence toward a common group estimate, more accurate response with iteration, and improved group response in contrast to face-to-face discussion. It is opinion that has been moved from a lower to a higher level of probable validity.[1]

Appendix B

The 220 individuals invited to participate represented the following groups:

1) local church pastors and lay people who had been members of annual conference or general agencies and/or members of the 1976 General Conference;

2) annual and jurisdictional conference leaders, such as chairpersons of agencies, conference lay leaders, presidents of United Methodist Women and United Methodist Men, district superintendents, and conference council directors;

3) general or denomination-wide leaders, such as members of the Executive Committee of the Council of Bishops, officials of the 1976 General Conference, and presidents, chief executives, and staff members of general agencies;

4) chief administrators of theological schools, colleges and universities, hospitals, and homes;

5) persons with special skills and expertise, such as theological professors, editors of church-related periodicals; and

6) research and planning specialists in the denomination.

One hundred ninety-eight persons agreed to participate, and 133 participants completed the process.

Notes

Chapter I
1. John Wesley, "The Law Established By Faith, Discourse II," *Sermons On Several Occasions, Volume III* as cited in *John Wesley*, Albert C. Outler, ed. (London: Oxford University Press, 1964), p. 230.
2. DeBois S. Morris, ed., *Perspectives for the '70s and '80s: Tomorrow's Problems Confronting Today's Management*, National Industrial Conference Board, New York, 1970, p. 1.
3. George C. Sawyer, "Mapping the Future: Planning Action Based on Coming Events," *World Future Society Bulletin* (March–April, 1979) World Future Society, Washington, D.C., p. 1.

Chapter II
1. *Religion in America: The Gallup Opinion Index, 1977–1978*, The American Institute for Public Opinion, Princeton, New Jersey, 1978, p. 24.
2. *Ibid.*, p. 25.

Chapter V
1. William Ramsden, *The Church in a Changing Society* (Nashville: Abingdon, 1980).
2. *ISR Newsletter*, Institute for Social Research, University of Michigan, Ann Arbor (September, 1979), p. 6.
3. *Ibid.*
4. Robert L. Wilson, "Where Did All the Money Go? United Methodist Expenditures in an Inflationary Period," *Research Information Bulletin* 12 (June 1, 1978), General Council on Ministries, The United Methodist Church, Dayton, Ohio.

Chapter VI
1. Warren Bennis, *The Unconscious Conspiracy* (New York: AMACOM Books, 1976), p. 149.

2. *Ibid.,* p. 153.
3. Richard A. Hunt, "How District Superintendents See Themselves and Their Work." A mimeographed report prepared for the Committee to Study the District Superintendency, The Division of Ordained Ministry, The United Methodist Church, 1979, Nashville, Tennessee.
4. Bennis, p. 157.

Chapter VII
1. Alexis De Tocqueville, *Democracy in America,* J. P. Meyer and Max Lerner, eds. (New York: Harper & Row, 1966), p. 3.
2. Daniel Bell, "The Revolution of Rising Entitlements," *Fortune* (April, 1975).

Chapter VIII
1. Walter Vernon, "The Growing Tribalism of United Methodism," *The Circuit Rider* (May, 1979).
2. Thomas Griffith, "Reshaping the American Dream," *Fortune* (April, 1975), p. 88.
3. *Ibid.,* p. 204.
4. John Scharr, as quoted in *Footnotes to the Future,* 8 (1979), No. 4. Futuremics, Inc., Washington, D.C., p. 2.

Chapter IX
1. Morris, p. 5.
2. Fred Polak, *The Image of the Future* (New York: Elseview Scientific Publishing Company, 1973), p. 300.

Appendix A
1. Morris, p. 5.